Lead with Your Heart

AND THE REST WILL FOLLOW

Cindy Tansin

Copyright © 2013 Cindy Tansin

All rights reserved.

ISBN-13: 9781492289562
ISBN-10: 1492289566

CONTENTS

CHAPTER 1	TAKING STOCK	1
CHAPTER 2	YOUR OWN WORST ENEMY	13
CHAPTER 3	CONQUERING LEADERSHIP FEARS	19
CHAPTER 4	LEADING PEOPLE	27
CHAPTER 5	LEADING CAUSES	35
CHAPTER 6	LEADING YOUR BUSINESS	41
CHAPTER 7	TROUBLESHOOTING	49
CHAPTER 8	GETTING YOUR MOJO BACK – MOTIVATING YOURSELF	59
CHAPTER 9	REINVENTING YOURSELF	69
CHAPTER 10	THE BALANCING ACT	71
RECOMMENDED RESOURCES		75
ABOUT THE AUTHOR		77

ACKNOWLEDGMENTS

I would like to thank my business coaches, Raymond Aaron and Ian Houghton, for inspiring me to write this book. They made me realize that I have important knowledge that should be shared, and they provided the tools and information I needed to turn that knowledge into a book. I am forever grateful to them both.

I also want to thank and acknowledge Jeff Shular. While I was in the process of writing this, many of the topics were reinforced through his teachings. He is one of the inspiring leaders who I have been fortunate to work with who has taught me a great deal in a very short time.

Lastly, I want to thank the many terrific people who have worked for me. They were very tolerant of my imperfections as I honed my skills as a leader, and were very generous in teaching me what I needed to know to be a strong and motivating supporter of their success.

Chapter 1

TAKING STOCK

---

*"You don't need to change the world;
you need to change yourself."*

Don Miguel Ruiz

Most leadership books give you a long list of dos and don'ts that are hard to remember and live by consistently on a day-to-day basis. They also tell stories about great leaders in history and business today and all the heroic things these great leaders did to reach the lofty positions of power they ultimately attained. Good leadership is actually much more attainable than many would have you believe. You only need to focus on two critical elements, and the rest, as they say, will follow.

The first is your ability to look at yourself in an honest and critical way. How do you think, act, and feel? What's important to you? Do you speak and act based on what's in your heart, or do you model yourself on how you think you're *supposed* to act? **When you are true to yourself, you set a great example, and you can be in a position to influence people.**

If you are *trying* to be someone or you are *acting* like someone, you can only get so good at the act. It will all seem empty to you at some point, and it will seem empty to those around you much sooner. The "magic" just won't work after a while, and you will only be sporadically or temporarily successful before your act requires a great deal of effort to sustain.

When you are true to yourself and to what's important to you, you can make a difference. Unfortunately, in most business environments, everyone tries too hard to emulate the "big dog" at the top. Everyone is afraid to act differently or to say anything that might cause him or her to stand apart. The problem with this thinking is that these kinds of safety nets are what cause so many leaders with great potential to remain impotent and invisible. If they don't stand out, they aren't noticed, seen, or heard. If they do stand out, they fear that it may be perceived negatively, and they could face possible criticism. It's a conundrum for many good people, and one that keeps most silent.

However, there is no way around the issue: you **must** take chances in order to excel and make a difference. You must dare to stand out and speak up. You must dare to voice your opinion. You must dare to be different when different is how you feel. If you don't, then you can only be as good as you can pretend to be, and your impact on others will be as lukewarm as your effort to be heard.

What's worse than not having the positive influence you crave is allowing your conformity to perpetuate the problem. When this happens, everyone who is under you tries to emulate you and satisfy you, but you can only be satisfied with your interpretation of the next higher-up's vision of what it takes to be successful. Hence, you contribute to a vicious cycle of talking heads whose sole purpose is to protect their turf and create clones. How boring and unproductive is that?

So the first step is to take stock of yourself. Take a good, long look and be completely honest with yourself. After all, no one else will know whether who and what you are on the inside matches whom or what you are trying to portray on the outside. The more you learn about what's really going on inside you, the more you will want to move in that direction and forget the false persona you've worked so hard to build.

Let's look at some self-examination questions. These questions will help you to align who you are with the things that matter most to you:

1. **What are your passions?** What do you love to do? What do you love about what you do? Whether you are in a junior position in the workplace or in a senior executive position, it is surprising how valuable this exercise is and how your answers can change over time. A good way to determine what you love is to ask yourself what aspects of your current job you find enjoyable, and, hence, relatively easy. These tasks come naturally to you and flow out of you with a minimum of strain and effort. What do you find yourself curious about and always wanting to dive deeper into? What have you done in the past that you have found satisfying? What are you naturally good at?

Make your list as long as possible. This serves two purposes: it gives you a reference point in determining future actions, and it gives you permission to feel good about various accomplishments and talents. This may sound odd, but what if you like to do something completely unsexy, like auditing? Guess what; that's okay! It's okay to love auditing. As long as it turns you on, that's terrific. That's exactly what you're determining with these questions.

2. **What are your goals in life?** Are there things you would like to work toward accomplishing? In other words, if money were no object and you never had to work, what would you do with yourself and your resources? What interests would you pursue? Discover and do these things. Strive for them, and you will get them. Believe that you should have these things, and take the actions necessary to put them into play so that you will get them.

We must not downplay what we consider our ultimate goals. If what you are doing feels good, and it earns you *enough* to keep you happy, and you are able to support your lifestyle, passions, and dreams, then bravo! Revel in it, and continue to refine it until you can't possibly get any better at it or get any more satisfaction from doing it. Go for it and enjoy! If, on the other hand, your goals are vastly different, consider what aspects of your current job will get you closer to that outcome. What can you aspire to achieve in your current occupation that will get you incrementally closer to your goal? Most of us have to take the building block approach, and there's nothing wrong with that. We grow along the way, we build along the way, and we lead others along the way. That's fantastic.

3. **What is the highest level you think you can attain?** This is very important, and I want you to think very carefully about your answer. It's a good idea to assess the result that might be within reasonable reach and to determine which actions will end in you doing something you actually *love*. It's like the old proverb: be careful what you wish for. You could be so myopically focused on an outcome only to wake up one day and ask yourself, *What was I thinking?* Believe me; I've been there.

I have to tell you an important truth that you may have heard but not believed: **Your only limitation is you. If you *think* you can only go so high, then you are right. If you think you can go higher, you can, and you probably will**. Conversely, if you think you will never be the CEO, make the top pay, hit your goals consistently, or any other desire, then you won't. Don't set your sights too low. Being the very best at what you love to do should be a conscious intention—not just an idea of something you try to do, hope to do, or think it would be nice to do. Once you *intend* to do something, you have set yourself up to make it happen.

This brings us to our second most critical element in leadership. **Once you intend to do something, the natural response is to take the steps necessary to *do* what you set out to do.** Set it in motion. Pencil out the first actions you can think of that will support your goal. Then take those steps and write out the next ones. That's all you need—believe, plan, and do. But always remember your ultimate goal, and ask yourself along the way if your actions support that goal, detract from that goal, or add no value whatsoever. When you do this, it is very easy to set yourself up mindfully for the success that you know you can achieve. This process also helps you to avoid setbacks.

How long will all of this take? I want you to realize your ultimate dreams, but it's important to remember that how determined and willing you are to make them happen, or how far these dreams are from your current reality, will determine how long it takes to get there. The goal is to get you to the place you ultimately want to reach and to enjoy the lessons and experiences along the way. Be strategic. What actions can you take *today* that will contribute to your *tomorrow*? If it doesn't contribute, then rethink it.

4. **Decide what you want to be when you grow up.** If you're still trying to figure this out, pick a destination that sounds good to you right now. That way, you're moving, growing, learning, and discovering along the way.

It's all good. The important thing is to have a destination in mind. Don't worry; it's not set in stone. If you change your mind along the way or you get to where you wanted to go and you still want more, you can always choose a new goal. This can be true for people who have achieved much in life as well as those who are early in their careers. Some of us come to a late realization that life is more than the defined box that we once drew around ourselves. If that describes you, then congratulations are in order. Identification of the problem is the first step toward solving it.

If you have no destination in mind, you'll end up nowhere. You will meander through life from one job to another—one relationship to another—in constant search of satisfaction from some elusive external source because you never took the time to think about what you really wanted. You just kept taking whatever fell in your lap or felt right at the time. This is exceedingly unsatisfying and doesn't lead to good choices. So pick something good and work backward to figure out what steps you can take *today* to lead you there. Even if that tomorrow is so grandiose or seems so far away and impossible, dream it and work toward it anyway. You may surprise yourself. When you align your activities to contribute toward your goal, you make deposits in your proverbial bank. As your "bank account" grows, you move *purposefully* toward seeing your dreams come to fruition.

5. **Be (or become) comfortable with who you are.** Who are you anyway? Many of us struggle with this question throughout our lives. If you haven't struggled with it yet, you're fooling yourself. I noticed two things early on in my career. First, most of the "successful" leaders in my company fit a profile. They had many of the same qualities, mannerisms, ideas, and actions. I knew I needed to be just like them if I wanted to be in the club, but there were also the anomalies.

   I remember Elaine T., a manager at one of our competing offices. Elaine was soft-spoken, had a huge heart, was thoroughly compassionate, and believed in people. What was particularly odd to me was that she was equally compassionate to all of her peers and sincerely tried to help them whenever they sought her out. Yet, she was always at the top of the performance rankings. She didn't talk, think, or act like any of the other "successful" leaders I'd ever known, and yet she was the most successful of them all. She was a puzzle to me.

   After spending several years trying to emulate the majority of leaders in my field and crawling up in baby steps, I started to ask myself what was wrong with me. I thought that maybe I just didn't have it. Everybody else seemed better at "it" than I did. I felt that I was never going to get ahead, but then I remembered Elaine. I remembered how successful and how different she was.

It made me wonder who I really was, since I wasn't good enough at what I was trying to be. I had gone so long trying to imitate others that I had never cultivated my own style and personality in my work. I concluded that I didn't feel comfortable acting like others. I never seemed to have the same eloquence of business speak that they had. I was always putting on a show and hoping that the show was wowing them. I was trying so hard to portray an image and believe it myself, and it just wasn't quite working. I was not breaking through or getting the promotions or accolades that I felt I deserved. And when I was put on the spot, I was nervous. Showtime always made me quake.

When I finally had a serious heart-to-heart talk with myself, I realized that I had no idea who I really was. I had no identity. I had no idea what my management style was or, for that matter, my true personality, beliefs, and inner wisdom. The bottom line was that I didn't trust myself. I was so caught up in trying to be just like my peers that I didn't realize that my peers were not so great at the game either. Once I realized this, I decided to let my barriers down (gulp) to see who emerged. I needed to find out who I was.

For starters, I decided that I didn't need a label. I didn't need to define myself through my results or through my occupation. I didn't need to define myself through my relationships, my family, my neighborhood, or the kind of car I drove. I am more than the sum of all these parts, and that's okay! I am a complex combination of unique qualities that make me my very own brand. I like that! And as it turned out, over time, so did my employees, my peers, my managers, my partners, my family, and my friends. Who'd a thunk it? I became much more successful when I let my guard down and started taking chances, speaking up, being different, and most of all, listening to my inner voice, my gut, and my own insatiable curiosity and demand for quality. It took a serious leap of faith, and at first, I didn't know where to start, but I just put one foot in front of the other and kept moving forward.

I learned that I am able do whatever I want to do in my own style, and do a damn good job at it, and I don't have to try to become something that I'm not to fit an image. In my case, I have always worked in conservative corporate environments. As I have slowly evolved, I have come to see that **trying to be what you *think* somebody wants you to be or what *you think* you need to be to perform a role is very limiting.** It's like wearing a girdle. You walk around as a very compressed version of yourself; your thoughts, ideas, and opinions are all compressed and predictable. When you do this long enough, you won't even realize you're doing it. It becomes part of your character. It ends up defining you, and once that happens, you're dead.

So back to the question of, "Who are you, anyway?" You have to be willing to dig to find out. Question, ponder, be open-minded, and trust your instincts. Maintain a level of healthy skepticism, even about what you are reading now, and check in with yourself often to decide if what you hear, see, or feel is *your* truth or someone else's truth that he or she is trying to sell to you. If it is, don't buy it. Take the girdle off. Breathe, believe, and be yourself. Now you are ready to soar.

6. **Do not be afraid. Instead of worrying about fitting in, being accepted, and being liked, concentrate on adding value, taking ownership and responsibility, and BEING HAPPY.** This is close to the most important advice I can give you. You can almost stop reading now, but don't—I want this to stick, and I want to drive this home a few times and in a few different ways.

    It is incumbent on *you* and no one else to make your working environment a better place to be. *You* need to set the tone. *You* need to set others free and allow them to find their own style to becoming successful. *You* need to nurture your flock, provide a healthy environment for them, and encourage them to grow, spread their wings, and discover their own way of adding value to your business and their own success.

Chapter 2

YOUR OWN WORST ENEMY

"You should tell yourself frequently, 'I will only react to constructive suggestions.' This gives you positive ammunition against your own negative thinking."

Jane Roberts

I will never forget coming home from the hospital, gazing down at my newborn daughter, and being simply amazed at what I had produced. As the days went by, her personality emerged, and I was absolutely astounded to discover that this little, barely-formed thing had a very distinct personality. This seemed like such a miracle and mystery to me. Where did this personality come from? She was just created!

My baby daughter was a person with a combination of characteristics that make her uniquely her. She would be influenced by many people and experiences along the way, but somewhere the essence of her would always be there.

What is the essence of you? You may have lost track of who you really are and only know who you've become. Take a moment to think about that. If you examined what your prevailing characteristics are, how would you describe yourself? Once you start becoming conscious of your thoughts and feelings, you should be able to identify whether you are an optimist or a pessimist, or maybe you already know—maybe you think pessimism is realism. Are you being realistic when you see a challenge as a roadblock? Isn't it just as realistic to see challenges as another facet of the game that you have to find a way to work with or around? If challenges are looked at as problems, deterrents, or reasons that you can't do something, then you might as well face the truth that you are being pessimistic.

This could be the hardest thing you do. It takes honest soul searching to find truth, and if you've built up layers of protection, then you have a long way to dig. If you find that negative aspects dominate your thoughts, then you can reevaluate whether there is another way to view and approach any given situation. Do this first in your heart, and then outwardly. Mostly, you need to resist the urge to deny that these negative, self-destructive thoughts and feelings apply to you. Everybody has them. The trick is to change your outlook so that you have fewer and fewer of them. Once you do that, you can really get somewhere.

We are addressing negative thoughts because they invade the soul like fast-growing weeds. They will take over and destroy you if you let them. You *cannot* achieve and sustain success and happiness if you have a negative outlook on life. It is impossible.

Here is an exercise and a test that will help you determine to what degree you may be suffering from negative self-think. Try this and see what you learn:

Exercise: Am I an optimist or a pessimist?

On a piece of paper, write the words Optimist/Positive in one column and Pessimist/Negative in another. For one full day, as you experience stressors and everyday activities, examine your thoughts about what just happened, and put a tick mark in the appropriate column. Remember to be conscious of your emotions and thoughts throughout the day. If doing this for a full day is too cumbersome, try it for just a few hours. You will learn how much negativity is part of your life.

Every tick mark in the Negative category represents a thought that has detracted from your happiness and, hence, your success. Your thoughts define you. If you have more tick marks on the negative side of the paper, then start working with yourself before addressing anything else.

Most negative emotions are subsets of one big one: Fear. Every negative emotion can be traced back to something you are afraid of: failure, destitution, abandonment, inferiority, and so on. Identifying a problem or a belief is the first step to solving it. If you discover a theme that stems from an irrational fear, or even a fear that stems from prior trauma, acknowledge it, accept it, understand it as something from your past, and allow yourself to heal. Forgive yourself for being fearful and for hanging on to your fears. Promise yourself that you will move on.

We don't need any of the negative thoughts and emotions that we carry around with us as personal baggage. They are doing nothing but weighing us down. All we have to do is *believe* in the possibility that what our minds tell us isn't necessarily true. The stressor causing the negativity can be looked at in another way because there is another perspective on the matter. Turn that thought into something positive or neutral, and feel the weight lift.

Practical Application

- Your thoughts guide your emotions. When your thoughts are negative, they produce either fear-based or self-esteem-based issues. Change your thoughts to positive ones, and watch these issues melt away.

- Act as though you belong. Otherwise, you won't, and your awkwardness will stand in the way of your progress. In leadership, it's important for others to be comfortable around you. Having appropriate dress does not have to infringe on your individuality. You need to look and act as though you fit in if you want to be taken seriously. **As a leader, you not only need to be comfortable with yourself, but it is respectful of others to make them comfortable with you**.

- Decide what to do and stick to it. Don't enter into anything halfhearted or half-baked. You've probably heard the saying, "If it's worth doing, it's worth doing well." Throw yourself in with gusto, and let it take you where it can.

- Keep dancing, and always have one eye open for things to build on. More importantly, never stop growing. Life will never become stale; you will always have something to look forward to, and the rewards will be commensurate with the efforts.

- Flow and momentum are very important in business. Stops and starts drain energy. Continual strategic activity and forward thinking are empowering and energizing.

- Listen to your intuition and act accordingly. When you actively check in with yourself for truth and validation, you can trust yourself to always do and say the right things. Thus, it's a confidence builder.

- **Take the time to be alone with yourself, and make it quiet, relaxed time**. This is important for rejuvenation and for the maximal conditions needed to gain insight and clarity.

- Form an alliance with leaders or those you aspire to be like. You are associated with the company you keep. Leaders and mentors you admire will be happy to share their ideas and thoughts with you. They like to help. It's amazing how few people take the initiative to ask questions or to follow through on the suggestions they are given.

Chapter 3

CONQUERING LEADERSHIP FEARS

"Defeat is not the worst of failures. Not to have tried is the true failure."

George Edward Woodberry

What if I can't deliver?

This fear stems from a lack of confidence and a feeling that outside forces are in control. Here you are a victim of your market, your pricing, your employees, your customers, your competition—anything and everything other than *you*. This fear is a symptom of lacking ownership. It takes a cool head to understand the attributes and actions necessary to step outside of your challenges and apply the tools in your arsenal to deliver results. The key elements here are *keeping a cool head* and *applying appropriate actions.*

Take ownership to become competent. In other words, don't panic. Figure out what you can do and what the most effective actions you can take are, and then take them. When you take ownership and take action, you lose the fear. **Becoming competent makes**

you confident. You can't help but become competent if you apply action with a cool head. **You become competent when you put your knowledge, skill, and experience *into action*.** To be competent, you must be good at what you do. You don't have to be perfect, but you should be better than most. And most importantly, *never* shut down.

What if I don't follow the herd and I'm perceived as weak or rebellious?

The more competent you become, the more confident you become, and the more comfortable you are with being you. People who follow the herd are a dime a dozen. They are the masses. You can be among the masses, or you can be a leader. Do you want people on your team to follow you blindly, or do you want them to think, to provide their ideas, to thrive, to grow, and to add to your success? The bigger fear here should be what happens when you *do* follow the herd. Can you stand by while your soul atrophies? It is incumbent on you to find a better way to grow yourself and to grow other leaders. **Your aim should be to make the herd strong, not to simply blend in**. Be a part of the group, but be an integral part, not just someone taking up space and breathing group air. Make a contribution!

What if I say something and it's taken the wrong way?

Without question, there is an art to speaking. Some people love to hear themselves talk, and you can count on them to always have something to say in a group setting. Some never speak, so you never know what's going on in their heads. There is a happy medium.

Surely, you have meaningful ideas, thoughts, and questions that are worth considering. However, not every random thought is worth repeating. If you fit into this group, then it would behoove you to apply filters. *Finish* the thought in your head before you blurt it out. Chances are that you will answer your own question or come to your own conclusion. Pause for a moment. Perhaps someone else has the same question, and it would be better to let him or her ask it.

As a leader, you must foster good communication skills. You should make it safe and collaborative for people to voice ideas, issues, and questions. Let others answer the questions to foster a variety of ideas for ways to approach the situation. Encourage everyone to voice his or her opinion by calling on the quiet ones from time to time and praising their suggestions and learning opportunities.

Chances are that if you have the fear of speaking up, you have been the victim of or witness to someone who has bravely made a comment and been shut down, or the comment wasn't received well. This can happen. There are two ways of dealing with it when it does.

First, don't let it stop you. If it keeps happening with the same person or in the same environment, address it appropriately, but don't let it stymie your creativity and productivity. Decide what you can learn from it, adjust as appropriate, and then carry on.

Second, don't do this to other people. You have felt the sting. Analyze what went wrong with the interaction so you can be certain to refrain from doing it to someone else in your next group situation.

What if I go out on a limb and it doesn't work?

Trying and failing says that you are willing to take chances. It says that you are creative. It says that you are willing to take action. It says you will *try*. Let's look at this from another angle. If you follow the status quo and do exactly what is asked of you and nothing more, you're showing others that you play it safe. Your actions say that you will never be better than average—you are a follower. You are telling others that you are not confident or creative.

Practical Application:

You achieved your current level of expertise by proving that you are competent in what you do. It is helpful to understand the skills and attributes it took for you to achieve your success thus far, because you can use these to build your success. This activity will help you to boost your confidence by acknowledging your competence. It will highlight the things you love about what you do, and it will help you to determine any gaps in development and the next steps of your personal growth.

On a piece of paper, write the following four questions:

1. Where do I want to go?
2. What will it take to get me there?
3. How am I contributing to this goal today?
4. What's left that I need to do?

Where do I want to go?

When you answer this question, take whatever pops into your head, and delve deeper into it to understand what your ultimate goal is. When I did this exercise, my answer was *security*, which meant financial freedom, independence, abundance, charitable giving, and teaching, growing, and nurturing others.

What is it going to take to get there?

Make this list as long as you can imagine. My list included things like paying off debt, saving, being highly creative, and managing time wisely; seeking administrative help, being accessible but empowering others to be self-sufficient, and being congruent and strategic in thinking; imagining the possibilities and acting on them, building my network, connecting people, and working with my coaches.

I would also encourage you to do research in this area. If, for example, you want to model yourself after someone, then dive in and find out how he or she lives and thinks. Find out what he has accomplished and what he did to get to where he is today. This can provide a useful roadmap. But don't think that you have to follow a formula. Create your own, but understand that seeing what others have done to get to where they are is very useful.

How am I contributing today?

Here you want to list everything you do in your daily life that adds to the outcomes above. You should be very gratuitous in this list. Give yourself credit for every little thing you do that leads to your ultimate goal. These are your strengths and your accomplishments. Acknowledge them and be proud of them. You have done good work.

What's left that I need to do?

Go back over the lists for the first two questions. Circle anything that you are not currently doing, not doing well, or could do better. This is your list of things to do. These items are holding you back from reaching your goals. These areas will give you the most significant lift when you improve them.

I strongly encourage you to do this exercise and to *write it down*. It is a proven fact that writing something down makes it stick, and it increases the likelihood that you will actually complete the task that you have set for yourself.

Summary:

If you apply these skills and practices in a consistent manner and stay open to new ways of applying these skills to enhance your current role, you can undeniably consider yourself competent. Now that you have acknowledged your competence, you have just increased your confidence. When you are confident, you have a head start on being a great leader. True leaders don't let fear dominate them or determine their actions. They act from the heart, trust their intuition, and gain respect and admiration for their fearlessness.

Playing it safe and hiding in the middle makes you invisible. When you hide, you deserve to be among the herd. In essence, you are telling yourself that you don't count, you don't exist, and you don't matter.

Lead with Your Heart

When you are at the top of your game, you are visible. Consistently being at the top makes you credible, but even so, you can't expect your results alone to speak for you. It's not just what you know, and it's not just who you know; it's also who knows you. Becoming known should be the goal of a competent, confident leader. You now have something to offer others. It's time to give back. That's what a leader does.

You can eliminate self-esteem-based fears when you:

- Believe in yourself
- Know that you are good, and know why you are good
- Know that you are capable because you have learned and applied your knowledge
- Know how much you have to offer
- Give up trying to control others, and instead teach them the skills they desire to learn, and then trust them to apply them. Your number one aim should be to build your team's confidence by building their competence.
- Act as though you belong. When you do this, you will feel much more confident in your ability to fit in.
- Listen to your intuition and act. Always go with your gut once you've trained yourself to listen to it. If it doesn't feel right, it's not. If it feels right, go for it!

Chapter 4

LEADING PEOPLE

"A leader is best when people barely know he exists; when his work is done, his aim fulfilled, they will say, 'We did it ourselves'."

Lao Tzu

So let's get to the heart of the book. You are already behaving like a leader by taking ownership of yourself and taking steps toward honing the skills necessary to carry out the sacred responsibility of leading others. Let's first talk about some of the **mistakes and pitfalls** that we should be wary of when leading people.

1. **We assume that since we have mastered a skill or achieved a level of personal success, we can and should lead others.** This is not a given unless we have some fundamental tenets under our belt. It takes more than just knowing the job to lead and motivate people. Sometimes the best leaders aren't familiar with the job at all, and the most experienced people at the job can make terrible leaders. Jobs can be learned and so can leading, but it is

definitely a process and a calling. Do not lead unless you plan to serve, support, and guide the people you lead. Otherwise, you will just torture them, and you will doom yourself to a life of stress and dissatisfaction that could turn you bitter, ruthless, and dead inside. Be brave and strong enough to acknowledge when you're not good at leading. **Management is not a rite of passage. It should be earned, and you owe it to the people who work for you to do a great job leading them.**

2. **We fail to learn from bad role models.** We dismiss them, suffer through them, and often let them demotivate us and impede our career progress. Dealing with negative energy is nothing new in business, but dealing with a boss's negative energy is the most challenging of all. However, we can learn some valuable lessons about motivation by observing how they demotivate others. We can learn what *not* to do from observing negative role models. It's best to look at them as a blessing instead of a curse. They present learning opportunities and act as builders of strength and character. If you can rise above your boss's negativity and succeed despite him rather than because of him, you will earn favor with him and become a better, stronger person— one who has learned some valuable lessons. Live through it, take what you can from it, and grow from it. Meanwhile, take stock of everything this bad role model is doing wrong so that you can make sure not to repeat his errors with your direct reports. Take solace in

knowing that the bad ones will not last long. They never do.

3. **We focus only on the results, the outcome, and the numbers, yet we do little or nothing to develop the skills and activities needed for success.** It does no good to be dictatorial about achieving results. When an employee is confused and doesn't know how to fulfill a given task, he needs collaborative instruction. When a goal or an outcome seems overwhelming, the only way to get past the inertia of panic is to put one foot in front of the other and know that a rhythm will develop, and things will fall into place as long as the quality and the right activities are there with each step. You have to set the pace by educating and guiding your employees onto the right path. If they choose not to follow, or they prove unable to do what you have taught them, then the results will speak for themselves. At least you can say with a clear conscience that it was not for lack of guidance.

4. **We tell people what to do instead of letting them learn from experience.** People learn better and are more likely to try things that they discover for themselves. We can show or tell people the winning approach to a situation, but if they haven't found the way for themselves, they won't use it, or they won't put their hearts into it. When asked, they'll say they tried and it didn't work. They won't have a sense of ownership or the same conviction they would have if they had come up with

the solution on their own. **As difficult as it is, leading people to a solution is considerably more effective than expecting them to follow your direction.**

5. **We buy in to everyone's drama about how hard it is to get the results.** This becomes an overriding mantra, and we lose faith in our belief that we have the ability to succeed. Our beliefs are always right, so what we believe is who we are. If we *believe* our challenges are bigger than we are, then they are. If we *hope* we can overcome the challenges, then our chances are fifty-fifty at best. And of course, if we really think we can't do something, then we won't do it. Don't buy into the roadblocks. Just deal with them strategically and watch them become less significant.

A Leader's Duty

As leaders, our challenge is twofold. **First, we have to motivate and manage ourselves. This means staying engaged, interested, and excited.** We have to manage our time carefully so that the majority of our time is spent helping people improve. This will produce much better results than being swallowed by meetings, conference calls, and e-mails. Then, of course, we have to motivate and guide our team members to keep them engaged, interested, and excited, which helps them manage their time properly.

As leaders, our responsibilities extend beyond ourselves, and even beyond the people who work for us. It is our role to build future leaders. We should lead by example and influence others to become better citizens, classmates, partners, family members, friends, employees, and employers. We should strive to be better employers, manage better companies, and be more responsible and valuable contributors to society. Our only boundaries are those that we choose to acknowledge. Otherwise, we can and should choose to take responsibility for every aspect of our lives.

Key points to remember:

- **Lead with the assumption that your people are doing their jobs, and be excited about their successes**. You are there to support them and make them more successful by helping them to develop their potential. Believe this and your words and actions will always be right. This is your professional purpose on earth.

- **Eliminate pressure in the workplace.** People just don't perform well under too much pressure. Some pressure, of course, is necessary and healthy. You must hold them accountable and hold them to a higher standard, but don't create an environment of pressure. Otherwise, in order to deal with the stress, they will shut down. They will go into full self-defense mode and focus all their efforts on not getting into trouble and telling you what you want to hear. Ethics can become a concern, and burnout is inevitable.

- **Be a motivator**. Motivation comes in many forms, but it is extremely effective in its most basic form. I'm talking about respect, honest concern for people's success, understanding their struggles and helping them cope, listening and responding, and allowing them to say what's on their minds without fear of retaliation or negative labeling. Respect also means giving honest and realistic answers to their concerns—not giving them the company line or the glossed-over answer, but the real deal. All the other stuff is icing on the cake. The contests, prizes, rankings, recognition, and motivational communications can add to the fun and shake things up, but these are pointless without the fundamentals.

- **Understand and address your employees' concerns**. No company is perfect. All have limitations. All have to weigh the needs against the resources and maintain profitability. The mindset of, "We could do so much more business if only we had _____" can lead to a very long and unending list. As a leader, you need to vet your employees' concerns and address those that have the most merit. For concerns with difficult solutions, lead your team to discover the solution or workaround with the resources they have.

  Do not let them use challenges as a crutch, but at the same time, do not underestimate their importance. If people are not given a voice, or if their suggestions or issues aren't addressed or taken seriously, they will stop voicing them. That's the first sign of death. No voice means no buy-in and no improvement for the business. This is a delicate issue that needs to be addressed; otherwise, it can easily turn into an unproductive whine session. Your art as a leader can turn these moments into productive learning sessions if handled sensitively, honestly, and positively. This is done by acknowledging the challenge, deciding what is and what is not in your control, determining the viable actions for the areas that are in your control, and working around the uncontrollable aspects. I can't stress enough how your ability to handle conflicts and challenges can produce the most defining moments in people's respect for you. Such moments also provide the best opportunity for your people to show their strength as leaders, because they will find ways to rise above the challenging circumstances.

- **Change your attitude**. You can't fake feelings—only behaviors. If you are harboring bad feelings toward someone, he or she will sense it loud and clear no matter how you behave. No one should be talked about "in confidence" to another. If you can't say something to a coworker or employee's face, then you are harboring feelings that are detrimental to his or her success. You must find a way to respect people as fruitful contributors to your business, or they will never become one. You might as well start the process to move them out, but beware; if that is your approach, word travels fast, and it demotivates even the most loyal and successful employees. They will soon wonder what will happen to them when they lose your favor. They will worry when they lose a peer who they enjoyed working with, and they will look for employment elsewhere. Conversely, if you have someone on your team who is poison, he or she is best handled decisively and affirmatively.

- **Believe in your team as if they're your children**. Care about them, build their confidence, build their skills, guide them, and support them. They rely on you for that. You are the most important person in their work world, and that's a very important world. Be a good parent, be a good boss, and be a great leader!

Summary

A leader should:
- Contribute to and share ideas
- Ask questions to determine the level of support needed, such as, "What's working for you? What are your biggest challenges?"
- Help eliminate barriers
- Continually reinforce the need to focus on goals and controllable activities
- Encourage, trust, and support your employees
- Add value
- Hold your team members accountable
- Don't give them a laundry list—just one or two next best steps to work on
- Keep it fun and interesting

Chapter 5

LEADING CAUSES

"If not me, who? If not now, when?"

John Dove, PhD

Leadership does not only entail leading people. Sometimes it means leading a cause. You can make a name for yourself by choosing to stand for something. Leading a cause shows your character, concern, and responsibility. It sets you apart.

When you align yourself with a cause, it says that you take a bigger outlook beyond your personal life, comforts, and job, and you take responsibility and ownership to make things better for the community at large. It's not something you do because someone asks you to or expects of you. Rather, you do it because you feel that you must. This shows character, and it is admirable. It is a sign of leadership because your actions go beyond what is expected.

Once you become aligned with a cause, you become the go-to person for that cause. Be aware, however, that it can be just as easy to become aligned with negative actions and ideas as positive ones. For example, if you show up late to meetings and appointments or miss deadlines, and you always have an excuse related to your outside activities, you become known as the person who is always late or who doesn't show. That becomes your brand. In a sense, this brand becomes your cause. Your cause is to show up when you feel like it, which may work for you, but it doesn't work for anyone around you. You have just committed a leadership crime and joined the league of followers who wait for direction and wonder why the good opportunities always go to someone else.

As a good leader, the kinds of things you want to be aligned with are operational excellence, employee satisfaction, and high customer service standards. Once you have decided what you are going to stand for, don't settle for anything less than optimum quality in these areas.

You don't have to be obnoxious about your cause. You're looking to become a leader who understands the importance of insuring that the work you produce in conjunction with your team meets the highest standards in your industry. Before long, you will find yourself setting the standard and being recognized for your delivery of excellence.

Another facet critical to leading a cause is to make it repeatable. A *cause* is something that you want to influence others to take up to make the world a better place. It is vital to model something that the average person can do. We want our causes to be repeated by as many people as possible so that we can improve standards in our community or company.

This endeavor is not about being competitive; it's about being altruistic.

If you want your cause to be repeated by others, develop some degree of expertise that others will notice and want to model. It takes commitment to truly understand, break down, and define a process that is both easily repeatable and effective. In the example of customer service, it could be something such as rewarding employees for notifying managers when they are unable to satisfy a customer completely. Most employees don't go beyond their job descriptions, and it never enters their minds to tell their bosses when they make a customer unhappy. However, the boss may never know that the employee needs help understanding managerial expectations or discretionary authority unless the manager is "lucky" enough to get a customer complaint.

A side benefit to leading a cause is that you often find that opportunities arise from your involvement with the cause. For example, you find a niche that you have developed expertise in, and now you can find opportunities within that niche and perhaps grow business enterprises such as consulting and keynote speaking or writing papers, articles, or books. This could be an excellent way to launch a business or propel a career.

Often, championing a cause means challenging the status quo to achieve improvement. This may not be met with fanfare, and it is usually not in the "safety zone" where nobody makes changes, and nobody gets noticed. Most people are comfortable with routine and predictability, especially if their routines take minimal effort or thought. Unfortunately, this leads to lack of growth and could potentially render you and your business obsolete. At best, it will only lead to mediocrity and thus invisibility.

It takes a brave person to stand up and say, "Something needs to change." Of course, tact, diplomacy, and timing in the way you make this pronouncement will make all the difference in how well your suggestion is received. If you don't have a better solution, then do not be that annoying person who is the first one to point out why something won't work or why something is a bad idea. If you are about to propose change, make sure you have given a lot of thought to how the change should unfold; then, be prepared to present your suggestion for improvement along with your identification of the need for improvement.

You add value to any company or team when you are brave enough to say when something is wrong or when change should be considered. The more thoughtful your ideas are, the more respected you will be for proposing them, and the more seriously you will be taken. It's easy to fade into the background when you are among people of title and prestige, and it is easy to speak just to be heard without any true substance behind your words. Neither of these are characteristics of a powerful leader. Choose your words, your cause, and your timing carefully. When your audience is ready and the topic is appropriate, your feedback will have the most impact. Sometimes you have to gently lead and prep the audience, and if you do this well, your listeners will realize that change is necessary, and they will be very open to your ideas.

Any improvement results from change, so do things the usual way until you perfect them, and then look for ways to expand and improve to keep them alive. **Growth comes from change**.

Summary:

1. Become an expert in your chosen area of specialization. Make this your cause and your brand.

2. Make your cause real and practical. When you are recommending a change in process, it needs to be repeatable. Often the most brilliant ideas are the simplest.

3. Make it something that you will genuinely enjoy delving deeper into. Don't specialize in something that you don't particularly enjoy, or it could become your curse. If you do, turn it into something you love. When your heart is in the game, the possibilities are endless.

4. Be the champion of change when improvement is necessary. Change for the sake of change is rarely very interesting, but it's worth experimenting. If you don't, you'll never have that next great idea.

Anybody can lead a cause. You don't have to be a Fortune 500 CEO. Anyone at any level can decide to stand for something, and in doing so, he or she will stand out. This is even more impressive when it comes from someone who is not high in the hierarchy, because it's not expected of her. That makes it a WOW. (This will be discussed in the following chapter.)

We should foster and encourage these behaviors in our employees, our children, our neighbors, and our friends. Think of what a great society we could build if more people spoke up and stood out to make *positive* change.

Chapter 6

LEADING YOUR BUSINESS

"Losers see barriers; winners see hurdles."

Mark McCoy, Olympic Gold Medalist

Differentiation through WOWs:

When it comes to running your business, what's important is creating WOW experiences. It's not good enough just to open the doors and sell stuff. Your products and services are not all that unique from your competition's. But how you deliver on the experience of buying your products and services makes all the difference in the world.

For starters, determine what the industry standard is for your goods and services and what your customers should *expect* to receive. These can be called minimum standards, but I call them roads to nowhere, and those roads have very steep inclines. When you are on such a road, you have to work hard for every sale and every win. Think of the outcome if you are not even delivering these minimum standards—you are on the downhill side of the road to nowhere.

So how do you stay on track and really thrive? Find some way to WOW people. If it's hard to do that with product differentiation, then you have to focus on service delivery. Ask yourself what you can brand as uniquely yours; then, put a stake in the ground and say, "I will deliver on this every time, and I will do it flawlessly." This is a differentiator, and it's a WOW, because no matter what else may go wrong in the process, you know that you will deliver this one thing without fail.

Now you can create buzz around your special form of delivery. You can make it a focal point with your employees. You can reward them, recognize them for their efforts, and do fun activities to keep them motivated. You can involve your customers by encouraging them and rewarding them to find employees who are *not* delivering on the promise. Once the word gets out, customers will come to expect that you will always deliver. They'll tell two friends, and they'll tell two friends, and so on.

Negative WOWs

The biggest killer of business is inconsistency. If only *some* of the people do things right *some* of the time, you don't have a WOW. So it's best to get the delivery of your WOW down to a science. Make it something that is simple to do repeatedly. Don't start the buzz or make any claims until you have it down solid.

Little things make the biggest difference

You don't necessarily have to come up with some big gimmick or giveaway to get people's attention. Sometimes an abundance of little things done right makes all the difference in the world. People are very forgiving when they know you are trying. You are allowed to make occasional mistakes or have occasional missteps when you go overboard *trying* to satisfy. Southwest Airlines did this with a sense of humor and friendliness. They were the first no-frills airline to herd everyone onboard like cattle, but at least they were lighthearted about it, and their light mood had a similar effect on their customers.

As another example, one day I went to a little lunch spot in Woodland Hills, California, named California Pita Grill. The first time I went, I stood in line with many others, and when I placed my order, the owner said, "Thanks for coming, Cindy; have a nice day." I didn't think anything of it until the second time I visited, and he greeted me by name when I placed my order. The third time I came, I noticed he was doing that with everyone, and I was truly impressed. We eventually got to talking, and it became like visiting a friend every time I went in. As if that wasn't enough to WOW me, I changed jobs and stopped eating there for some time because I no longer worked nearby. I returned one day, two years later, stood in line, and the owner greeted me with a warm, "Hi, Cindy, welcome back!" I was astounded. It was just a tiny little thing, but it made a big impression on me, as I'm sure it did with all the other customers who came regularly. By the way, I also noticed that his employees were *always* smiling, which told me his niceness wasn't just an act.

Listen to the customer

We all hate it, but the best source of information about what needs to be fixed is through customer complaints. Sure, there are those who use the complaint channel simply as a way to get things free or cheap. But almost every complaint has something behind it. The biggest mistake you can make is to disregard complaints or fail to act on them when you hear about them.

No matter how petty a complaint may seem, there is something to be learned from it. If it's a "people" complaint versus a "thing" complaint, then taking that complaint to the accused accomplishes two important things. First, it gives the employee an opportunity to contemplate the situation through the customer's eyes. This helps the employee learn how the situation could have been handled better, or how he might have been able to alleviate the complaint by doing or saying something different.

Second, by going to your employee with the complaint, it tells him or her that you take every complaint seriously. If your employees are aware that they will have to explain themselves to you whenever a customer situation is escalated, they will be much more thoughtful when handling similar situations in the future.

Likewise, "thing" complaints should not be taken lightly. These usually serve as warnings that your basic operations or products are failing in some way. If your infrastructure is not grounded and in good working order at all times, you could find yourself in some serious trouble, reputational or otherwise, unless it is properly addressed and corrected. **Your customer service agents should be rewarded for escalating every fixable complaint to someone who is**

empowered and committed to getting it fixed. This is a commitment to quality. This will make you stand out. This is truly important.

Listen to the employee

Customers don't only come to us with problems, although we often remember and dread problems the most. Often they ask us about additional products and services, and if it's something we can't provide, we should consider ways that we can. It's good to get your people attuned to these suggestions and questions and to encourage them to pass these along to management. A quiet employee who simply does his job and never voices his opinion or his customers' opinions is the bane of every employer. Unfortunately, such employees are the bulk of the workforce. Employees who don't strive to go beyond their duties simply don't care, or they think you don't care. If they don't care, then you're dead. If you know that they *do* care, but they don't put forth the effort because they think *you* don't care about their suggestions, then you're really dead.

Many employees will not say anything because they have not been encouraged to do so. They have somehow been led to believe that being uninvolved is just the way it is in the business world, or they once voiced a concern to someone who didn't acknowledge the validity of it or didn't do anything about it, so they vowed never to do that again. Worse still, maybe they voiced a concern to someone who simply defended the problem. This causes people to shut down and shut up. If this is your management style, you will hear no further suggestions from your employees. They will not try to fight for the business because they will be convinced that their suggestions don't matter. They will simply do their jobs. Rewarding employees for actively providing ideas, suggestions, and red flags only makes sense.

Go beyond communicating to connecting

The best employee is one who attempts to have an actual conversation or connection with a customer. An example of this happened to me recently. I was in a chain drugstore. The customer ahead of me paid for his order, and the cashier pulled out his receipt and said, "Oh look, you got a five-dollar coupon that's good on anything you buy. Why don't you go back and get something else so you don't forget to use it?" The customer was delighted. He said, "Keep my bag; I'll be right back."

I was impressed too. I commented to the cashier, "That was a good deal." He rang up my order, pulled out my receipt, and said, "Well, look—you have one too. I must be lucky today!" So, naturally, I went back and bought some more stuff. The other customer and I left with big smiles on our faces, and we will be certain to visit *that* drugstore again.

It can be challenging to find people who smile easily and are good at initiating conversation. When you do, leverage this by putting them in a position to do what they do well, and try to get them to train others to duplicate their behavior. Sociability can be learned. It's harder for introverts to master this skill, but it's definitely possible with practice and a desire to do well.

Change leads to opportunity

You must be comfortable being uncomfortable. You cannot grow in your comfort zone. If you want to stretch your mind and move your business forward, you have to stretch yourself. Stop going through the motions. Start looking for opportunities to propel your business forward. Look for risks to take. Do calculated experiments, but never mess with your existing successful strategies—just throw in a few ideas to see where they will take you. If your endeavor takes you nowhere, it's no big deal. Stop and reroute. If it takes you somewhere, explore deeper, work out the kinks and the details, and then fly. These are what make life worth living. There is nothing more satisfying than discovering a winning strategy.

Sometimes it's just a little twist on an old theme. That's awesome. My favorite trick is to take other people's good ideas and make them better. Hone your radar for good ideas, and then let your imagination take over. If it already worked for someone at one level, imagine what adding a trick or two will do for you. *That* is fun!

Chapter 7

TROUBLESHOOTING

"In the crush of our information overload age, the greatest luxury isn't money. It isn't fame. It isn't even attention. It's time."

Noah St. John

Dealing with stress

As a leader, you take on a lot of responsibility. It seems the more responsibility you take on, the more that is asked of you. The more that is asked of you, the harder it is to say no. You eventually find yourself working long hours and sacrificing more and more of your own time and needs to get everything done. On top of this, I'm asking you to champion change, lead people, and drive your business forward! Whew, it can be exhausting just thinking about it.

But does it have to be that way?

What if we had just enough stress to keep ourselves stretched? What if you looked forward to the new challenges of each day? Wouldn't it be invigorating, motivating, and just plain fun if you faced the challenges head on with an action plan in hand, ready for anything?

It's only when we are overwhelmed, underequipped, and overextended that we start to get that ugly stressed-out feeling. If it isn't alleviated in short order, the feeling becomes chronic, and chronic stress leads to illness and burnout. We all know that stress is the leading cause of illness. So what are the keys to early warning, treatment, prevention, and ultimately a healthy prognosis?

E-mail: One of the biggest stressors of all

No matter how fast you plow through them or how much you multitask, you never get close to emptying your e-mail inbox. Because of this, you find yourself constantly drawn to them, ridiculously believing that today will be the day that you magically reach bottom. The only problem is that e-mails have a multiplier effect. For every one you send or respond to, you get two, five, or ten back. It's a form of torture. You have better odds winning the lottery than you do of actually emptying your e-mails and keeping them clear.

So this is the first symptom. They taunt you. Even when you resist all temptation and snub them, like when you actually take a vacation day, you are overwhelmed with worry about what emergency might need to be addressed. You dread that it's going to take you twice as long to get through your e-mails if you leave them until the next day. You foolishly think that if left undisturbed, you will be able to shoot out a whole bunch and just get them done. But people start responding, and before you know it, you've been sucked in, and three hours of your life have vanished before your eyes.

If having someone screen your e-mail is not an option, here are some of the tricks I've picked up along the way that might be of help to you.

- Tell the people who are most important to you (your customers, employees, and business partners) that you will do your best to respond to time-sensitive requests as quickly as possible. However, they have your permission to call you any time they need a timely answer and have not heard back from you within an appropriate period. This will allow you to be responsive without living in fear of missing a critical time-sensitive message.

- Prioritize your time. If you see an e-mail that you want to read but simply don't have time right then, move it into a Read Later folder. When you have free time to think, digest, and enjoy it, go through the folder at your leisure.

- If you see something that requires a follow-up of some sort, and thus you don't want to delete it because it isn't fully resolved, move it to a Tasks folder, or save it to a Follow-Up folder. Either way, it's safe and it's saved, but for now, you've read it and dealt with it, so you can get it off your plate. You will know that the Tasks or Follow-Up folder needs to be checked regularly.

- Other than that, read, respond, delete, and move on. If it's from someone important, like your boss, you might want to save it, just in case, in an archive folder. Otherwise, dump it!

- Don't use the most productive time of your day reading e-mails. You should have hallowed hours that are used for doing activities that increase your business. Pick a time that you will check e-mails, and let your team and business partners know your routine so that they don't expect you to be connected 24/7.

- I saved the best advice for last: **only allow so much time in your day for dealing with e-mails.** E-mails can be business killers. They are critical to our businesses, but they take so much time away from them. It's amazing how much more efficient a phone call can be. Use e-mail as a backup in case the person you need to talk to is unavailable when you call—because *hopefully* they're busy doing actual business!

- One final note on e-mail from the perspective of the sender: As a leader, recognize the need to keep outgoing e-mail minimal and concise. If you need to go into a lengthy diatribe or a list of instructions, e-mail is not the correct forum for this. Meetings or conference calls are much more effective.

"On" Time

You might be conducting a meeting, presenting at one, speaking on a conference call, conducting a review, or coaching, analyzing, and giving feedback on a project. Whatever the case, these activities require you to be "on." When it's over, you get a quiet moment, and you crash. You are spent. You go home, uncork the wine, put your feet up, and veg out for the rest of the evening until you go to bed early, wake up early, and start all over again.

When you're in the moment, and it's going well, the performance high is quite enjoyable. This is especially true if you've been able to spend some quality time putting together your thoughts and preparing for the event, or you have stretched your mind from engaging in the event. How you choose to carry the exhilaration forward is entirely up to you. It's very easy to control your mood when you give it conscious thought; you don't have to end with a crash and burn. Prolong that energetic level of readiness forever by giving yourself permission. You just have to decide that you will remain in your energetic state.

The best example I can give of this is when I attended a two-day business seminar over a weekend by a renowned business coach. When he first came out to start his presentation, he said that he had just returned from Antarctica with his daughter where he finished a two-day race across the coldest, most desolate stretch of land he'd ever seen. He had literally just gotten off the plane and landed in Los Angeles a few hours earlier, and here he was giving his presentation.

I was astounded and thought to myself, sarcastically, that the seminar was going to be a waste of time. He would give some tired speech, and that would be the highlight.

But I couldn't have been more wrong. He presented for two days solid, and his energy level remained the same from the beginning to the end. He never showed signs of tiredness or strain.

To add to my astonishment, even though I had gone through a typically exhausting workweek before attending this very full two-day weekend seminar, I left with more energy than when I started. I never went back to believing that I would or should crash and burn after a long "grueling" day again. This is because I changed from being an observer and a slave to my life to being the active, willing director of my life. Since this was *my* life to design and run, I wasn't going to waste my time any longer doing meaningless activities that only drained my energy. Instead, I focused on meaningful activities that contributed to my success and, therefore, fed my energy engine.

In the process, I learned and realized that crashing and burning after exerting a lot of energy is unnecessary, and it tells us that what we've been doing does not feed us and work for us. We've been focusing on our interpretations of what we're supposed to be doing.

Rethink your life, and if you conclude that you're doing it wrong, be energized from the good feeling you get taking action to set yourself right. It's exhilarating.

Performance Anxiety

Let's face it; one of the biggest stressors for any leader is when performance results are not up to par. Everybody has off moments. The best time to address them is before they are full-blown, because by then you will be in full panic mode. It's extremely difficult to get out of panic mode. It's as if customers can sense stress coming out of your pores, and that's because they can. You can definitely read when people are off their game. They tend to be off in everything: the things they say, their looks, and their behaviors. They can't seem to get anything right. There's only one way to turn this around.

First, to illustrate my point further, there is a theory coined by Noah St. John concerning the inner game and outer game of success that perfectly describes what is happening here. In his theory, he describes two people playing golf. One has never picked up a golf club in his life but he has the utmost confidence, walks right up to the ball, and is certain he will get a hole in one. The other has been playing golf for years at the professional level, but for whatever reason, he does not have his head in the game that day and can't seem to get a good shot no matter what he does. Both play a terrible game but for different reasons.

The first player did not have his outer game together. He had the confidence and belief in himself and his ability to learn and score immediately, but he had no practical application to draw from; thus, he was not ready to jump straight into a serious game. The second player had fine-tuned skills and experience, but his own lack of self-esteem and belief in his ability sabotaged the game for him. He had his outer game under control, but not his inner game.

When you have both your outer and your inner game together, you have the potential for limitless

success. Concerning performance anxiety, determine whether the fault lies in your outer game or your inner game. Perhaps it's both. Only you can determine this. However, if something is lacking in your performance, it's one of the two. It's easy to start with the outer game and determine whether you've done all the things you need to do and taken all the necessary steps to have a the appropriate quantity of activities with a high quality of skill. If you can honestly say that you have applied all the necessary actions, then it's time to explore your inner game and face the fact that you truly believe that you cannot achieve what you desire.

Many books have been written on the subject of how to adjust your attitude, and I highly recommend them to even the most positive, pragmatic person. Everyone can learn something new, and we all have our moments of doubt—even the most confident people in the world. All it takes for our sense of worth to crumble is for our bosses, our spouses, or our children to say one little hurtful, insensitive thing to us. If your self-respect comes into question frequently, the psychological buildup and damage can become so ingrained that you don't even see it or feel it anymore. But until it is acknowledged and dealt with, it will stay inside, and everything you do and say or don't do and don't say will be done out of fear.

So please, do yourself a favor and analyze whether your inner self or outer self is off. If it is the inner self, and it doesn't bounce back quickly with conscious attention and effort, then please understand that you have some work to do in this area. Outer-game issues are much more straightforward, which makes them easier to deal with. You can fix what you know is broken. So identify the issue and take appropriate action to address it. Even the act of identifying and addressing is a stress reliever. When you know you are in the middle of a fix, you cut yourself some slack, and that's a good thing. It's the first step toward reversing the curse of performance anxiety.

If you are unclear of the crux of your inner issues, then the best way to sort them out is through meditation, introspection, and honest self-evaluation. The best way to deal with outer issues is to face the problem head on and explore all the ideas you can come up with to address and correct the situation. I also suggest researching other options and ideas, seeking the help of a coach or mentor, and reaching out to peers and business partners who are willing and able to help you. You may not discover the answer per se, but you will become clearer and gain some traction. By addressing the problem directly, you will feel better about yourself, recover your self-esteem, and lay the groundwork for a turnaround.

Chapter 8

GETTING YOUR MOJO BACK — MOTIVATING YOURSELF

"When we are no longer able to change a situation, we are challenged to change ourselves."

Viktor E. Frankl

Ever have those days—sometimes weeks—when your battery is just drained? If this happens on occasion and you bounce back up, that's normal. If it prevails, and you just aren't getting any juice out of what you do anymore, it's time for a deeper look. I've never been a believer in taking a pill to make troubles go away. In fact, I advocate *against* masking or even treating the symptoms. I am a believer in finding the *cause* and then acting accordingly.

Without taking the trouble to understand the *true* source of your doldrums, chances are that you will just carry on day after day, mindlessly going through the motions with very little heart or effort behind your actions. Your success, accordingly, will be hit and miss, or just miss. If you let this go unexamined for too long, it can lead to troubles associated with having too much time on your hands combined with too little stimulation.

When we feel burned out, we simply need to stop what we're doing and assess where we are and where we're going. Did we stray off our path somewhere? Is the road traveled not offering the same allure that it once did? Are things not working the way they once did? Perhaps everything has become too routine and comfortable. We have to be real with ourselves if we want to lead a fulfilling life of forward movement. Lulls are natural and normal, but if they go on too long, they can start a negative cycle that becomes harder and harder to break.

I am dealing with this issue on a basic level in this book. This is a book about business and leadership. But don't downplay the importance of psychology, mental health, and spirituality in every endeavor in life. We don't stop having spiritual and emotional needs just because we have jobs in corporate environments with bottom-line responsibilities. We are human beings first and business leaders second. Therefore, we *must* take care of ourselves, including our motivation levels, our spirituality, and our emotional wellbeing.

With that said, let me give you the practical primer. Since you are a reader, you are self-motivated, and you know how to seek guidance and advice independently. I encourage you to look deeper into this subject, and as a starting point, I have provided many great recommendations in the appendix. Meanwhile, here are the basics, the most important of which are the following:

What we think, we are. Our thoughts affect our beliefs, our truths, and our realities. It is not the other way around. If you *listen* to your thoughts throughout the day, you will discover that you have a variety of positive and negative thoughts in between a lot of gibberish. As leaders, typically we outwardly show our positive side and only let our guard down around a trusted few. Your *thoughts* have no guard and no filter. They are true to you no matter what persona or character you present to the world. In fact, there's a good chance that if your mojo is gone, it's because your thoughts and your outward personality are out of sync. You are not feeling or believing what you are attempting to portray.

It is very practical to take serious stock of your stream of conscious thoughts when your spirits are down. *Listen* to them. Make note of the trend. What are you spending most of your time mulling over? Are your thoughts consistently negative? Is there a recurring theme? What kinds of themes have you been seeing in your dreams? It's quite easy to stop negative thinking midstream and redirect it, but the tricky part is to be aware of it. For example, if you have a thought such as, *Oh God, I hope I don't blow this presentation*, you have just raised your chances exponentially of blowing the presentation. You have set yourself up to stumble. The positive version of this thought is, *Here we go. This is going to be good.* If you think you have to look or talk a certain way in order for people to take you seriously, you have increased your chances exponentially that people will *not* take you seriously. In other words, your doubts and fears will have become more real than actual reality. It is a self-fulfilling prophecy. Hence, what we think, we are.

What we believe is true. If we believe, for example, that our goals will be difficult to attain, then they will be. If this tends to be your mindset, you've set yourself up for struggle. You have prepared yourself for the long, hard climb, and now you must climb it. Conversely, if you take the actions necessary to hit the numbers instead of stressing over how hard they seem, then you are set for an upturn. The optimist, in this example, doesn't waste mental energy thinking about how hard it is to make her goal; she's busy making it, thus setting herself up for success.

In this case, another word for beliefs is *excuses*. **When you make excuses, you are vocalizing your belief in your lack of confidence to do what is necessary to achieve your goals.**

Let's look at another example. You would really like to earn a higher pay and get a promotion. If your tendency is to create a list of reasons why this will be hard to accomplish, or you worry that other people are likely to be considered before you, then what you *believe* is that you are not deserving of a promotion.

If you decide instead that you need to make a positive move in your career, and you want to ready yourself for the future, you will take the necessary steps to make meaningful, noticeable contributions. You will research the position you covet and learn the skills needed to excel in it; you will learn the history of the business; you will let people know what you are aiming for by seeking their help and input. When the desired position (or something like it) becomes available, you will have raised your credibility and the likelihood that you will be considered. Most importantly, you will go into it prepared and confident because of all the work you've done, and you will *believe* that you are worthy of the promotion, which will significantly increase your likelihood of getting it.

Hence, what we believe is true. For the person who believes there are many "reasons" that it will be next to impossible to get the job, it *will be* next to impossible for them to get it. However, the one who believes that he is ready and right for the position *is* ready and right for it.

What we feel is a result of what we believe. Our emotions come from our beliefs. **Whether we are feeling happy, light, confident, and in control, or depressed, distracted, angry, threatened, or bored, the root causes of these emotions are our beliefs**. Our beliefs about ourselves, and about the situations we find ourselves in, manifest themselves as *feelings.*

Let me give you an example. You meet a new peer or business partner at work, and you size him up. You tend to look for things about him that you are going to like, or you look for things about him that you are not going to like. You're likely to be oriented in one direction or another. Whichever way it goes gives you some indication of your thoughts and beliefs about *yourself.*

If you are insecure about your own self-worth, you will immediately look for the negative in others. If you find yourself in this category, you might be saying to yourself that this is a load of crap—you know an idiot when you see one. But ask yourself why you are so critical and judgmental. Stop for a minute and do a gut check. Breathe deeply, close your eyes, empty your thoughts for a moment, wait for the calm to settle, and ask yourself if it could *possibly* be true that because you are insecure, you feel threatened by others, and thus you don't like competition, or you hold some other version of negative self-think. If the answer is yes, it is possible then you've just had a revelation. Now you have something to work with because you've just been honest with yourself. This is the start of everything.

In this example, whatever we *believe* about this person, or about any given situation, will dictate how we *feel*. When we look at the good in a situation or person, we will *feel* good. When we see the bad in any given situation or person, we will feel bad.

Our beliefs drive our behaviors. Let's go back to our earlier example of the two people trying to get a promotion. The person who believes that it is nearly impossible to get a promotion thinks he has to wait for a million prerequisites to be met before it will happen. What steps do you think this person will take to get the promotion? Most likely none, or at least not enough to make a difference. People with this mindset will continue to do what they have been doing all along and wait bitterly for someone to tap them on the shoulder and realize how great they are. Or they will apply for positions and arrive unprepared, with no compelling stories or endorsements to make them stand out. The prepared person is likely to come to the interview with some very creative, workable ideas and compelling stories. His or her efforts will be noticed.

If you *believe* that you will not hit your goals, then you will likely go through the motions of what you are "supposed" to do, or you will be discouraged and keep finding ways to prove that your excuses for not being able to make your goals are true. It will be more important for you to be right than for you to be successful.

In either case, you can see that these negative beliefs are a trap. They set you up to fail. They erode your momentum and your spirit. They make everything seem hard and futile. And they are lies. The proof is the people who *do* get the promotions and who *do* make their goals. What makes them so special is that they *believe* in themselves, and so can you. The only difference between you and them is that they did not let negative beliefs cloud their judgment and their determination to *take the necessary actions to make it work*. It is that simple.

Our behaviors drive our results. The most important determinant of our success starts with our mindset, but it ultimately depends on our behaviors. Our actions ultimately bring about change, growth, and results because our mindsets are either the cause or the deterrent to our actions.

For example, as a business leader, you already know that certain actions are critical to running your business. This is your mindset. You may plan your days to facilitate prioritizing your most meaningful activities. However, you may let circumstances drive you by being sucked into reading e-mails, being consumed by time-wasting activities, and letting hours, sometimes days, get away by being reactive and doing nothing to propel your business forward. Which person do you suppose will be more successful?

The person who takes the necessary actions to succeed *will* succeed. The more halfhearted your behaviors and efforts are, the more halfhearted your results will be.

Three Elements of Success:

If you have found yourself lacking in drive—your mojo is gone and you are in a lull—then something happened to your passion. You had it once, or maybe you only *thought* you had it. Maybe you truly had it, but circumstances have changed. Any way that you look at it, passion is the key to drive. Sometimes it takes going through the motions (fake it until you make it) to kick passion into gear. Sometimes that's not enough. This is where you have to be honest with yourself.

Step One: Find your passion.

You might have to convince yourself to rise above your currently unpleasant circumstances. You might also have to take stock of your life and decide whether this is a meaningful bump in the road and you can retrieve your passion, or if it's time to move on. Only you can know the right answer. It can sometimes be helpful to confide in a friend, family member, or confidante; however, I have found that the only one whose opinion really matters is *you*. You have to trust yourself. If this is a new concept to you, buck up. But if you are the leader that I expect you are, then you understand what I'm saying.

If you want to get your passion back, you can start by contemplating what you love about what you do, and then immersing yourself in activities that you know will give you that sense of joy and satisfaction. I don't advocate running from your problems, but be smart enough to realize when the walls are coming down. If that is the case, then it's best to get out while your image and self-esteem are still intact. Go when your gut tells you that it's time. But make sure you have that heart-to-heart talk with yourself first. There are always options. Explore every one before making any decisions that you might regret later.

If you're exercising your passion, and you've just lost some of your oomph, you can get it back. However, if you don't have the heart to reinvigorate, then move on.

Step Two: How do you reinvigorate passion?

Let's assume that you are doing what you want to do, but you are simply in the doldrums. Things aren't working or feeling right for you anymore. You've lost your rhythm and hit a dry patch. You need to examine *how* you do what you do. It is likely that a better approach is needed to reinvigorate your business. It's time to do some spring-cleaning of your process. It's time to think about self-development and improvement. It's time to take your game to the next level. That will definitely put a spark in you.

Step Three: Do it.

Once you determine the better approach, take the necessary actions, and put what's in your head into play. Do something to turn your situation around. You will be astounded at just how quickly it does turn around. The positive outcome was there all along. It just needed *you* to decide that it was the path you wanted to take, and it needed you to plant your feet on that path and walk in that direction. The rest simply unfolds for you along the way.

The main thing is to identify that there is a problem, make a fair assessment of the problem, consider the possible outcomes, and then *take responsibility* by acting on it and doing something about it. **Life doesn't happen *to* you, it happens because of what you create through your thoughts, your beliefs, and your actions.**

Chapter 9

REINVENTING YOURSELF

"It didn't happen to you; it happened for you."

Dr. Leonard Coldwell

So let's explore the other side of the coin now. We have talked about when you are in the right situation but the wrong state of mind and how you can go about correcting your course. Here we're going to talk about being in the wrong situation but the right state of mind, i.e. the exit strategy. Usually, some big eureka moment happens that knocks you back to your senses, and you realize that something is undeniably wrong in your current situation. Whether this situation was unforeseen, inevitable, or caused by your own "mistake," if it resulted in a wake-up call, then do yourself a favor and see it for the gift that it is, despite the fact that it feels like a sudden rude awakening that what you thought you had all figured out, you were wrong about. How could something that started out so right turn out to be so wrong? Sometimes it just turns out that way.

If you are "lucky" enough to have one of these moments in your lifetime, then you are lucky enough to have learned that life is much bigger than our little worlds. We've been looking at our lives through a narrow hole and thinking that this was all that mattered, but it's not. Life is huge, and it has so much to offer. It's okay to take refuge in the bigger, quieter, and more profound world of ours. It's okay to have quiet moments of thinking and not thinking. It's a good idea just to exist for a while—to experience without trying to make something happen. Let life just happen while you observe and try to understand how all of these new experiences feel to you. Watch your emotions come, go, change, wax, and wane. You'll be left with a better understanding of what really matters to you.

Once you decide what moves you, you can start to rebuild. Now the process becomes much like the steps for getting your mojo back. Now it's time to get down to basics. Ask yourself what your passion is, what you want to do, and what you need to do to accomplish it. Determine how you can expand on what you know or have done thus far in your career, and apply this knowledge to something new. Keep your mind wide open and look for opportunities to make a change. They *will* present themselves, and you will see and find them when you are ready. They could present themselves as something completely new and different or something very similar with a new spin. Either way, they are a gift from God that you invited and recognized, so now it's time to accept the gift and act on it.

Chapter 10

THE BALANCING ACT

"You can have it all. You just can't have it all at once."

Oprah Winfrey

If you have balance in all areas of your life, you have fulfillment. But how do you have balance in all areas of your life? Why is it that, for the people who have it, it comes so easily, and for those who don't, it's so elusive? I would be willing to bet that the "lucky" ones have had their trials and gone through their own transformations. The following are some of the universal words of advice they would give:

Don't sweat the small stuff (and it's all small stuff).

Richard Carlson was a genius when he came up with this concept. The title says it all. Stress will kill you, but what's magic is that *you* have total control of what stresses you and what doesn't. If you *decide* that you are not going to let something (or someone) get under your skin, and you refuse to give "it" any energy or credence by thinking about it and getting annoyed with it, then you are on top of the situation. Don't let stupid stuff derail you. There will always be stupid stuff to deal with. That's life. You are way bigger than any of it.

Cut the cord.

If you find that certain people are dragging you down or relying on you for everything, then I strongly suggest that you find a way to gently cut the cord and let them go. You must realize that you are not doing them any favors by carrying them along. They are dead weight to you, and because they are adding to your burden, they are part of the problem, not the solution. The extra weight that you are bearing is not helping them. They are not getting better because of your control over their situation. When you think about that, I'm sure your answer will be that they are not gaining by depending on you; they are losing. The only way for them to get better is for them to become responsible and self-reliant. So, if overreliance on you is part of the problem, let the weight go. Release it. Set it free. Set yourself free. You will each find equilibrium when you are allowed to breathe.

Set boundaries.

I fully believe in finding ways to help others whenever possible and whenever appropriate. But help is not always appropriate. If you are a giver, this is a particularly hard concept to grasp. If you have already found balance, then you are reading this and nodding your head vigorously. No one should be expected to be all things to all people. It's not possible, it's not realistic, and it's not feasible. We can't try to be perfect! Don't ever stop trying to be damn good, but perfection is not mandatory or recommended. The closest I've found to perfection so far has been in a dog or in nature. So, when you have those moments of human imperfection, accept them, forgive yourself, admit your mistake, learn from it, and take steps to make things better. That's it. There is no better formula. But most importantly, don't continually overextend yourself because you don't know how to say no. For God's sake, say no once in a while. It won't kill you.

Have some offsets.

Nobody can be "on" 24/7, and nobody should be. We all need downtime, so build it in, and make it a priority. Plan for it and plan around it, and make your time all about you. Little breaks are great, but give yourself a big break every now and then. It may feel like a big sacrifice, but it's not. You sacrifice a whole lot more by not resting, because your morale, your mojo, and your effectiveness will start to wane. Give yourself power by doing big and little things that make you feel better. And most importantly, plan ahead. This makes the anticipation and the enjoyment all the greater.

By now, you have discovered that this book is not only about what you can do for the world, but what you can do for yourself. I firmly believe that being an altruistic leader of your community and a part of something bigger than you are is a worthy goal. But I have learned that all the personal sacrifice in the world is for naught if there isn't some gain, satisfaction, and love for yourself too. It is equally important to receive gracefully the love, accolades, and gifts that the world has to offer so you can be bolstered and give them back in spades.

This book is about you, dear reader, and everything you are and hope to be. I am rooting for you to be the person who rises above the rest and helps others along the way. I'm rooting for you to have a happy, healthy, abundant, and productive life. I give this encouragement to you, and I ask you to pass it on.

Please share your stories of success and/or your challenges with me and my other readers on my website at cindytansin.com. I wish you all the greatest success and happiness in your lives, and I trust that you will accept the baton that I am handing you and lead those around you to their best and highest existence.

Good luck and vaya con dios.

RECOMMENDED RESOURCES

Books:

Working Out, Working Within, by Lynch and Huang

Stepping Up: How Taking Responsibility Changes Everything, by John Izzo

Blink: The Power of Thinking Without Thinking, by Malcolm Gladwell

Creative Visualization: Use the Power of Your Imagination to Create What You Want in Your Life, by Shakti Gawain

Teleseminars:

The Aware Show, with Lisa Gar
theawareshow.com

From Heartache to Joy, with Eram Saeed
Fromheartachetojoy.com

ABOUT THE AUTHOR

Cindy Tansin is an entrepreneurial leader who has dedicated her career to finding better ways to succeed in business through personal growth and compassion. Her revolutionary approach is particularly appealing to middle managers who can be overwhelmed by demands and whose aspirations can sometimes feel unattainable. She has inspired many people to challenge the status quo and to grow both personally and professionally.

Her book, **LEAD WITH YOUR HEART and The Rest Will Follow,** addresses building leaders by promoting self-satisfaction, balance and personal growth as the key ingredient to creating a thriving, compassionate, productive business environment. She believes that it is equally important to feed and nurture oneself and others as human beings first and employees/customers second. A catalyst for growth and evolution, she has dedicated her career to teaching others how to develop their natural strengths, connect with others, and use their ideas and actions to positively affect their community. Her techniques have proven very successful in increasing sales, employee retention and talent development.

Cindy Tansin

Cindy Tansin has a depth of experience in senior leadership roles and has seen a lot of change over the last decade. Early to sense changing trends and with an unquenchable thirst for learning how to maximize personal and professional growth, she has been an avid student of meditation, yoga, energy transformation, creative visualization, and laws of attraction. She is a pioneer in applying many of these principals to business and helping to develop a new generation of business and thought leaders.

Cindy Tansin is a very involved author, manager, mother, and community leader.

Contact Information
To contact the author or to book a speaking engagement, write to info@cindy tansin.com

Visit Her Website
www.cindytansin.com

www.ingramcontent.com/pod-product-compliance
Lightning Source LLC
Chambersburg PA
CBHW051221170526
45166CB00005B/1988